Nic's Lunchbox

Mouth-watering lunch for kids who love to munch!

By Nicholas Brockelbank
With photos by Nigel Beach

SCHOLASTIC
AUCKLAND SYDNEY NEW YORK LONDON TORONTO
MEXICO CITY NEW DELHI HONG KONG

Hi, Nic again, I'm still cooking!

Nic's Cookbook was great fun for me to write, and it got lots of fantastic reviews. When I launched it in October 2012 the bookshop sold out in 30 minutes: 120 books sold in such a short time, I felt very proud!

Nic's Cookbook also received international recognition, winning the Gourmand World Cookbook Awards 2012 Best Fundraising, Charity and Community Cookbook in the Pacific Region.

I'm at intermediate school now, and everybody there seems to know me because I'm a bit famous from writing Nic's Cookbook, and being the Bow Tie Ambassador for the Muscular Dystrophy Association. Some of my friends at school enjoy having a ride in my power chair!

It's been amazing to get so many encouraging comments for my first cookbook and I was really excited to be asked by Scholastic to write another one. Nic's Lunchbox has some of my favourite lunchbox and party recipes. One of my favourite recipes in this book is the Sushi Sandwich, and I also love the Chocolate and Marshmallow Slice.

I donated half of my royalties from Nic's Cookbook to the Muscular Dystrophy Association and I'm really pleased to be able to help out again with Nic's Lunchbox.

Thanks to everyone who supported my first cookbook; I hope you enjoy Nic's Lunchbox.

Nic Brockelbank

Nic and Scholastic NZ are donating 50% of their royalties from sales of this book to the Muscular Dystrophy Association.

Nic Brockelbank with Judy Bailey, MDA Patron and Bow Tie Ambassador.

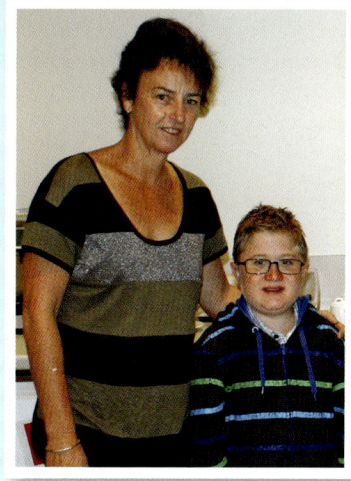

Nic Brockelbank with Dame Susan Devoy, MDA patron and Bow Tie Ambassador.

The vision of the Muscular Dystrophy Association (MDA) is that people living with a neuromuscular condition have unrestricted opportunities to achieve their full potential and live life with less boundaries.

I met Nicholas recently as part of my work as Patron of the MDA. He and I were promoting their annual fundraising appeal. It's not always easy for people to put themselves out there when they have a rare condition like Nic's. He is such a great example of a person not letting his condition, Muscular Dystrophy, define him. He is an MDA member, has appeared on television and won TVNZ's *Good Morning* show's Kids' Cook Off Competition, appeared on Attitude TV and still found time to regularly fundraise for the association.

Often neuromuscular disorders can be debilitating, not only for those diagnosed but also for their families. It's important to remember what a huge role support and guidance plays in helping MDA members. The association is a New Zealand organisation set up to provide specialist information and support services unique to people living with neuromuscular disorders.

Without these vital services MDA members would be pretty isolated. As a registered New Zealand charity, the MDA relies on the funds raised to operate. We appreciate Nic Brockelbank's generosity enormously, and thank Scholastic for their support of the MDA by donating proceeds from each sale of this wonderful book!

And please do enjoy Nic's great recipes … he's a star!

Judy Bailey

MDA PATRON AND BOW TIE AMBASSADOR

www.mda.org.nz

Congratulations, Nic, on the publishing of your second cookbook. What an awesome achievement. I am in awe of your talent, especially since I have four sons and they avoid the kitchen at all costs!

Your personality and passion for food and cooking shines through your books. It is inspiring to see you showcase your talent and we are delighted that Scholastic has helped to share this with everyone. You are a magnificent ambassador for MDA, demonstrating that we all have gifts and talents, and that nothing can stand in your way if you really love what you do.

I look forward to trying some of your new recipes, and following your future. I have no doubt that we will continue to be inspired by your efforts in and out of the kitchen.

Dame Susan Devoy

MDA PATRON AND BOW TIE AMBASSADOR

In 1988, during a 53-day trek covering the length of New Zealand, Dame Susan Devoy raised $500,000 for the Muscular Dystrophy Association. This year she has returned with the goal to raise $1 million. Shortly after this book's publication, on 27 October 2013, the MDA will be asking New Zealanders to get behind Dame Susan to assist her in raising both awareness and crucial funds for those Kiwis living with neuromuscular conditions. To get involved and follow the progress visit www.musclemiles.co.nz.

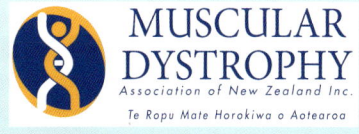

contents

Savouries

Lemony Chickpea Dip	6
Tuna Wraps	8
Nachos with Salsa	10
'Ham' Burgers	12
Cheese Biscuits	14

Always wash your hands before cooking

Pizzas, Sammies and Snacks

Sushi Sandwiches	16
Pizzas	
Tomato and Pesto	18
Spaghetti and Ham	19
Smoked Salmon	19
Sandwich and Lunchbox Fillers	20

Sweets

Chocolate and Marshmallow Slice	22
Mini Fruit Jellies	24
Pear and Boysenberry Pies	26
Nut-Free Muesli Bars	28
Kids' Carrot Cake Muffins	30

Difficulty Rating:

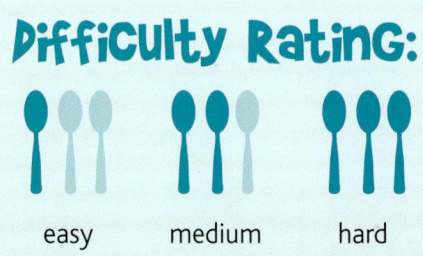

easy   medium   hard

Basic Cooking Terms

Dice

Sift

Spread

Measurements Glossary

Liquid or Dry Measurements:

tsp – teaspoon
One level teaspoon is about 5ml.

dsp – dessertspoon
One level dessertspoon is about 10ml.

Tbsp – tablespoon
One level tablespoon is about 15ml.

Liquid Measurements:

mls – millilitres
There are 1000mls in 1 litre.

Temperature
C = degrees Celsius

Dry Measurements:

g – grams
There are 1000g in 1 kilogram.

Length:

mm – millimetres, cm – centimetres.
There are 10mm in 1 centimetre.

Nic says:
Our pet rabbit, Jack, loves my vegetable scraps!

Lemony Chickpea Dip

MAKES ABOUT 2 CUPS

EQUIPMENT

- Can opener
- Food processor
- Chopping board
- Small sharp knife
- Sieve
- Measuring spoons
- Citrus juicer
- Serving bowl
- Rubber spatula

This can be made ahead of time and stored in the fridge in an airtight container.

1. Juice the lemon.
2. Drain the chickpeas and, if you're using them, sundried tomatoes. Cut tomatoes into small pieces. Peel the garlic.
3. Place in a food processor with all the other ingredients.
4. Process until combined. Add a little water if necessary; the dip should be a smooth paste, not dry.
5. Refrigerate for at least one hour.
6. Serve with pita bread and/or vegetable sticks.
7. **EAT!**

Ingredients

420g can chickpeas
2 Tbsp oil
2-3 Tbsp water (if needed)
1 garlic clove
3-4 Tbsp lemon juice
½ tsp paprika
¼ tsp salt
OPTIONAL:
4 sundried tomatoes
TO SERVE: Pita bread cut into triangles, vegetables cut into sticks for dipping (e.g., carrot, capsicum, cucumber)

TIP:

Some brands of canned chickpeas are softer than others; try a few to find which you like.

DID YOU KNOW?

Chickpeas are a good source of protein, especially for a vegetarian diet.

Savouries

nic says:
You can put this dip in a small container in your lunchbox with stuff to dip in it.

Gluten-free option

Eat with vegetable sticks instead of pita bread.

Savouries 7

Tuna Wraps

SERVES 4–6

EQUIPMENT

- Sieve
- Can opener
- Large bowl
- Measuring jug
- Measuring spoons
- Mixing spoon
- Chopping board
- Small sharp knife
- Knife for spreading
- Plastic wrap

Ingredients

½ cup cottage cheese
½ cup cream cheese
220g can crushed pineapple in its own juice (not sweetened)
185g can tuna in spring water
1 Tbsp sweet chilli sauce
2 spring onions
Salt and pepper to taste
3-4 large square Middle Eastern style wraps

Tuna filling can be made ahead of time and stored in the fridge in an airtight container.

1. Drain the cans of pineapple and tuna.
2. Finely chop the spring onion stalks, throwing away the root and coarse dark green end.
3. Place everything in a large bowl and mix until well combined.
4. Spread this mixture evenly onto the three wraps.
5. Roll each wrap up firmly.
6. Wrap in plastic wrap and store in the fridge until ready to serve.
7. When ready to serve, remove plastic wrap and cut into 2–3cm slices.
8. **EAT!**

Dairy-free option

Replace cream cheese and cottage cheese with 400g can of creamed corn.

nic says:

This yummy tuna mixture can also be spread on crackers or put in a sandwich with lettuce, tomato or grated carrot.

8 Savouries

Nachos with Salsa

SERVES 4

Ingredients

420g can whole peeled tomatoes
3 fresh tomatoes
1 tsp oil
1 clove garlic
½ small red onion
½ tsp ground cumin
Salt and pepper to taste
OPTIONAL:
½ small capsicum
½ tsp chilli paste
Small handful of fresh coriander or parsley
TO SERVE:
75g cheese (e.g., tasty, cheddar or edam)
175g packet corn chips (nachos)

EQUIPMENT

- Medium frying pan
- Garlic crusher
- Can opener
- Mixing spoon
- Grater
- Chopping board
- Small sharp knife

The salsa can be made ahead of time and stored in the fridge in an airtight container.

1. Peel and finely slice the onion. Peel and crush the garlic. Chop the fresh tomatoes into 1cm chunks.

2. Heat oil in frying pan.

3. Add onion, garlic and cumin to the pan and fry gently until onion is clear.

4. If you're using capsicum, remove seeds and dice finely. Add it to the saucepan. Add the optional chilli paste now, too, if you want to use it. Fry gently until capsicum is soft.

5. Add the canned tomatoes and juice. Mash up the tomatoes in the frying pan, and then add the fresh tomatoes.

6. Heat the mixture until boiling, stirring often. Simmer gently for ten minutes or until the juice has evaporated and the salsa has thickened, then remove from heat to cool.

7. Once the salsa has cooled, finely chop coriander or parsley (if you're using it) and stir it in.

8. When ready to serve, grate the cheese. Pack the corn chips and cheese in a different part of your lunchbox from the salsa, or, if serving at home, the cheese can be melted onto the chips under the grill (use a heat-proof serving dish for melting the cheese).

9. **EAT!**

10 Savouries

Gluten-free option

This yummy lunch is gluten free if served with vegies or gluten-free corn chips.

nic says:
This salsa isn't too spicy, and you can eat it like a dip with vegetable sticks.

Did you know?
Salsa is the Spanish word for 'sauce'.

Savouries

'Ham' Burgers

SERVES 4

EQUIPMENT

- Frying pan
- Chopping board
- Spatula
- Small sharp knife
- Knife for spreading
- Measuring spoons

Ingredients

4 baps or burger buns
4 ham steaks
Lettuce
2 tomatoes
4 Tbsp mayonnaise
Butter or other spread
OPTIONAL:
2 pineapple rings
2 gherkins

1. Cut the buns in half.

2. Thickly slice tomatoes and gherkins (if you're using them).

3. Preheat frying pan to medium and then add ham steaks. Cook at medium temperature for a few minutes on each side (the steaks will heat through and go a little bit brown on the outside).

4. If you're eating the burgers straight away, place each ham steak on the bottom half of each bun, then carefully stack lettuce, tomato, gherkin and/or pineapple on top of each ham steak. Top each salad stack with 1 tablespoon of mayonnaise, then add the top of the bun.

5. If you're making the burgers for later, cool the ham steaks and store the ham and salad ingredients in the fridge until ready to use.

6. When ready to eat or pack your lunchbox, assemble the burger.

7. **EAT!**

12 Savouries

nic says:
Unlike regular burgers, these still taste good when eaten cold. Can you imagine eating a cold cheeseburger for lunch? No thanks!

Savouries

Cheese Biscuits

MAKES ABOUT 50 BISCUITS

EQUIPMENT

- Measuring scales
- Sieve
- Measuring spoons
- Large bowl
- Grater
- Mixing spoon
- 2 oven trays
- Rolling pin
- Small biscuit cutters
- Oven mitts
- Cooling rack

Ingredients

1 cup flour (plus extra for rolling)
150g tasty cheese
150g butter (cold, straight from fridge)
3 Tbsp milk
½ tsp paprika
Salt and pepper to taste

1. Preheat oven to 180°C.
2. Sift flour into large bowl with paprika, salt and pepper.
3. Grate cheese and butter and add them to the bowl.
4. Add milk to bowl and mix all ingredients together. Add a *tiny bit* more milk if the mixture is too dry. (Be careful not to make the mixture too wet and sticky.)
5. Lightly sprinkle flour onto a clean benchtop or chopping board.
6. Place mixture onto floured surface and knead. (This is folding and pressing the mixture to form a dough). The warmth of your hands will soften the butter, helping all the ingredients to stick together.
7. Sprinkle the rolling pin with flour and roll the dough to ½–1cm thick.
8. Cut out the biscuits with the biscuit cutters. I used stars and rabbits this time.
9. Lightly sprinkle flour on the baking trays and place the biscuits on the trays, leaving 1cm between each biscuit.
10. Cook for 8–12 minutes until golden and bubbly, and then remove from oven. Leave for 5 minutes and then place on rack to cool.
11. **EAT!**

Savouries

nic says:
These are great to take to school for lunch. They make yummy party food too.

HOW TO
Knead Dough

Sprinkle a small handful of flour onto a board so the dough doesn't stick.

Push the dough forward firmly with the heels of your hands, and fold it back upon itself.

Continue doing this until the dough is slightly springy.

TIP:
These biscuits stay fresh for at least a week in an airtight container.

Savouries 15

Sushi Sandwiches

SERVES 2–3

Gluten Free

Ingredients
- ¾ cup short-grain sushi rice
- 1½ Tbsp sushi vinegar (rice vinegar)
- ¼ tsp salt
- ¾ Tbsp sugar
- 2 sheets nori (available from the International section of most supermarkets, or from Asian supermarkets)
- 2 eggs
- ½ spring onion
- 1 Tbsp mayonnaise
- 1 carrot
- ⅛ cucumber
- Salt and pepper

OPTIONAL:
Smoked salmon slices

EQUIPMENT

- Sharp knife
- Chopping board
- Medium saucepan
- Small saucepan
- Measuring cups
- Measuring spoons
- Peeler
- Grater
- 2 small bowls
- Fork for mashing
- Knife for spreading
- Dinner plate or tray
- Bamboo sushi mat
- Medium-sized bowl

The rice and the filling can be made ahead of time and stored separately in the fridge in airtight containers.

1. Wash the rice in cold water and drain.

2. Put the rice in a medium saucepan with 1¼ cups of cold fresh water and bring to the boil.

3. Turn down the heat, cover the pot and simmer the rice for 12 minutes. Wiggle the pan every few minutes to stop the rice from sticking to the bottom. Remove from the heat and leave the pot to stand for 10 minutes with the lid on.

4. While the rice is standing, put the eggs in water in a small saucepan and bring to the boil. Turn down the heat and simmer gently for 7 minutes, then drain and cover with cold water.

5. Combine the sushi vinegar, sugar and salt, and stir until dissolved.

16 Pizzas, Sammies and Snacks

6. Gently stir the vinegar mixture through the rice then spread the rice out on a plate or tray to cool.

7. When the eggs have cooled, peel them and put into the small bowl. Mash the eggs with the fork, add the finely sliced spring onion, and then season with salt and pepper. Add the mayonnaise and mix well.

8. Peel and grate the carrot and slice the cucumber into thin strips.

9. Spread the egg mixture evenly over one of the nori sheets, sprinkle with the grated carrot, then lay the cucumber on top. If using smoked salmon, lay this on top of the cucumber.

10. Spread rice over the other nori sheet.

11. Place the plain rice-covered nori sheet, nori side up, over the one covered in egg mixture.

11. Lay the bamboo rolling mat across the top of the nori sandwich, and gently press down so that the nori is even and smooth.

12. Remove the bamboo mat, wet the knife and cut the nori sheet into four squares, then cut each square in half diagonally. Each nori 'sandwich' makes eight triangle-shaped pieces.

13. **EAT!**

Option

You can use capsicum instead of the cucumber, or use the filling for the Tuna Wraps instead of the egg and salmon to make a tuna sushi sandwich.

nic says:
Keep your hands wet while working with the rice; it's really sticky!

Did you know?

The word 'sushi' actually refers to the rice, which has been seasoned with vinegar, sugar and salt.

Pizzas, Sammies and Snacks

Pizzas

MAKES 8 SLICES

Ingredients

For all pizzas:
1 large pizza base
75g cheese (e.g., mozzarella, tasty, cheddar, edam)

Tomato and Pesto Pizza:
1 Tbsp basil pesto
2 medium tomatoes

Spaghetti and Ham Pizza:
220g can spaghetti
50g sliced ham
½ cup canned pineapple pieces

Smoked Salmon Pizza:
1 Tbsp tomato paste
50g smoked salmon pieces
¼ cup cream cheese

EQUIPMENT

- Cheese grater
- Chopping board
- Knife for spreading
- Small sharp knife
- Oven tray
- Oven mitts
- Large knife or pizza cutter
- Can opener (spaghetti)
- Measuring scales (salmon)
- Teaspoon (salmon)

1. Preheat the oven to 200°C.
2. Grate the cheese.
3. Add whichever topping you prefer …

Tomato and Pesto Pizza:
A. Spread the pesto onto the pizza base.
B. Cut the tomatoes into thin slices and spread them over the pizza.
C. Sprinkle the cheese evenly over the top.

Spaghetti and Ham Pizza:
A. Chop the ham into small pieces and drain the pineapple.
B. Spread spaghetti onto pizza base and then cover with cheese.
C. Spread ham and pineapple over the top.

TIP:
If you like, you can make these using pita breads or English muffins.

Smoked Salmon Pizza:
A. Spread the tomato paste onto pizza base.
B. Arrange the pieces of salmon on top of the paste.
C. Dollop teaspoon-sized portions of cream cheese on the paste.
D. Sprinkle the cheese evenly over the top.

4. Place pizza on the oven tray.
5. Bake in the oven for 8–10 minutes until the cheese is bubbling.
6. Remove, allow to cool slightly and then cut into wedges.
7. **EAT!**

Pizzas, Sammies and Snacks

nic says:
Pizzas make great lunchbox food and can be made ahead of time and stored in the fridge.

Pizzas, Sammies and Snacks

Sandwiches and Lunchbox Fillers

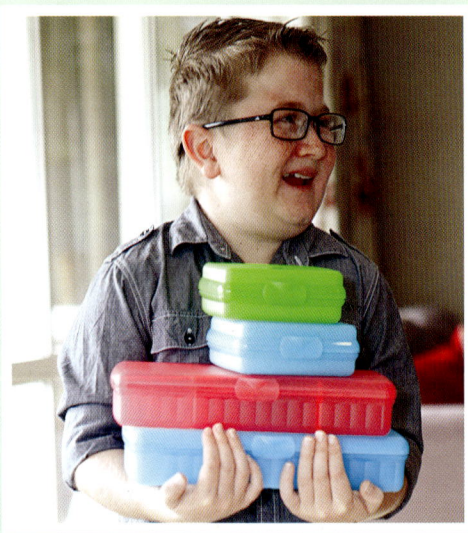

Sandwich Fillings (some of Nic's and his friends' favourites)

- Cheese and Marmite (a Kiwi classic!)
- Mashed hard-boiled egg mixed with mayonnaise (on its own or with shaved ham)
- Cream cheese and jam
- Peanut butter and sliced banana (if you put the peanut butter on both pieces of bread, it helps to keep the banana fresh)
- Tinned salmon, drained and mixed with mayonnaise (on its own or with sliced cucumber)
- Tuna Wrap filling (see p.8) and lettuce
- Grated cheese and grated carrot mixed together
- Sliced avocado and tomato, with pastrami (pat dry the tomato with a paper towel first if you don't like soggy sandwiches!)
- Cold corned beef with pickle
- Leftover roast meat (e.g., chicken, beef, pork) with relish or mustard

Nic says:

In summer, it's a good idea to keep your lunch in an insulated bag. If you freeze your drink bottle overnight and pack it in with your lunch, it will keep your food fresh for longer.

Remember

Do not put nuts or peanut butter in your lunch if there is a nut ban at your school because nuts can cause some people to have a nasty allergic reaction.

Pizzas, Sammies and Snacks

Great snacks to put in your lunchbox:

- Cherry tomatoes
- Corn chips
- Raw vegetable sticks (e.g., carrot, cucumber, capsicum)
- Rice crackers
- Whole boiled eggs (don't peel until lunchtime or you'll stink out your schoolbag!)
- Home-made popcorn (with a light sprinkle of salt or icing sugar)
- Dried fruit (e.g., cranberries, sultanas, apricots)
- Nuts or seeds (e.g., almonds, walnuts, hazelnuts, pumpkin seeds, sunflower seeds)
- Fruit cut into chunks (these can be stuck onto kebab sticks)
- Leftover sausages cut into bite-sized pieces

Tip:

Use frozen slices of bread to help to keep the food in your lunchbox fresh – they'll be thawed by lunchtime!

HOW TO Peel an egg

Gently bang the egg on the bench to crack the shell around the middle.

Peel a strip of shell off where you've cracked it.

The shell comes off really easily this way! Older eggs peel more easily.

Pizzas, Sammies and Snacks

Chocolate and Marshmallow Slice

MAKES 28 PIECES

EQUIPMENT

- Medium saucepan
- Mixing spoon
- Shallow non-stick baking tin (about 28cm x 18cm)
- Sharp knife
- Measuring cups

TIP:
This can be stored in an airtight container in the fridge for up to a week – if it's around that long!

Ingredients
- 50g butter
- 180g marshmallows
- 200g dark chocolate buttons
- 2 cups rice bubbles
- Non-stick baking spray

nic says:
This is not for every day, but it's a DELICIOUS sweet treat or party food!

1. Spray baking tin with non-stick baking spray.
2. Place the butter, marshmallows and chocolate buttons into the saucepan and gently melt over a low heat while stirring. DO NOT BOIL.
3. When melted, remove from the heat and stir in almost all of the rice bubbles, saving about ¼ cup.
4. Put the mixture into the tin and spread evenly. (The easiest way to do this is with wet fingers, as it is a sticky mixture.) This needs to be done quickly, as the mixture will start to set.
5. Sprinkle the last rice bubbles over the top of the slice.
6. Once cool, put in the fridge to set.
7. After 30 minutes in the fridge cut into pieces approximately 4cm x 2cm. If you are having trouble cutting it, carefully run the knife under hot water to heat the blade, this will make it easier to slice.
8. Return to the fridge to set further.
9. **EAT!**

Gluten-Free Option
Use gluten-free marshmallows and gluten-free rice bubbles.

Sweets

Mini Fruit Jellies

MAKES 4

EQUIPMENT

- 4 small containers (about ½ cup capacity, preferably with lids)
- Can opener
- Small sharp knife
- Chopping board
- 2 small bowls
- Sieve
- Fork
- Mixing spoon
- Measuring spoons
- Small measuring jug
- Kettle

Gluten Free

Ingredients

410g can fruit in juice

2 tsp gelatine

100ml water

Juice from can of fruit, made up to 200ml with extra fruit juice (e.g., orange, apple, pineapple juice)

1. Open can of fruit and drain with sieve, saving juice in small bowl.

2. If necessary, cut fruit into bite-size pieces and divide evenly among the four cups.

3. Place gelatine into the other small bowl. Put the kettle on to boil, then carefully add 100ml of boiling water to the gelatine, mixing with a fork until all the gelatine is dissolved.

4. Top up the saved juice from the can to 200ml with other fruit juice, then add to gelatine and hot water. Stir until well mixed.

5. Pour the fruit juice and gelatine mixture evenly into the four small cups, covering the fruit. Set aside to cool.

6. Once cool, cover and place in the fridge to set.

7. **EAT!**

TIP: You can use whatever canned fruit you like best, e.g., pineapple, peaches, fruit salad.

24 Sweets

nic says:
You can count these jellies as one of your 5+ a Day!

Pear and Boysenberry Pies

MAKES 8

EQUIPMENT

- Small saucepan
- Small bowl
- Measuring spoons
- Can opener
- Sieve
- Fork
- Pastry brush
- Small sharp knife
- Chopping board
- Baking paper
- Oven tray
- Oven mitts
- Spatula
- Cooling rack

Ingredients

- 410g can pears
- 425g can boysenberries
- 1 Tbsp cornflour
- ¼ tsp ground ginger
- ½ tsp ground cinnamon
- 4 sheets frozen, ready-rolled puff pastry
- 1 egg
- 1 Tbsp water
- 1 Tbsp caster sugar

The filling can be made ahead of time and stored in the fridge in an airtight container.

1. Preheat the oven to 220°C (or 200°C for fan-forced).

2. Drain pears and boysenberries, saving the liquid from the tin of boysenberries. Chop the pears into bite-size pieces.

3. Mix cornflour into 2 Tbsp of the leftover boysenberry juice to form a paste. Set aside.

4. Place fruit in a medium saucepan. Add spices and enough of the boysenberry juice to cover the fruit. Heat to a gentle simmer.

5. Add the cornflour and boysenberry paste to the fruit in the saucepan, stirring continuously while the sauce returns to the boil. DO NOT STOP STIRRING, otherwise the sauce will go lumpy.

6. Reduce heat and simmer gently for 2–3 minutes. Remove from heat and cool completely

7. Thaw pastry sheets on the bench. Cut each sheet in half lengthways. Place some of the fruit mixture onto one half of each piece of pastry, leaving 2cm around each edge.

8. Fold the plain half of the pastry over the fruit half to make a square, and use the fork to press all around the edges of the pastry. You need to do this firmly so the pastry will stay closed while the pies cook.

9. Use the fork to poke small holes in the top of each pie (to let out the steam when cooking).

10. Break the egg into a small bowl with 1 Tbsp of water and mix with fork to combine. Brush over top of each pie and sprinkle lightly with caster sugar.

11. Bake in the oven for 12–15 minutes until the pastry is golden and the filling is hot.

12. **EAT (WHEN COOL)!**

nic says: These can be eaten hot (don't burn your mouth!) or cold. Keep in an airtight container in the fridge.

Sweets

Sweets 27

Nut-Free Muesli Bars

MAKES 40

EQUIPMENT

- Measuring scales
- Measuring cups
- Measuring spoons
- Small saucepan
- Small bowl
- Large mixing bowl
- Mixing spoon
- Shallow baking tin
- Baking paper
- Oven mitts
- Large knife

nic says: If you want to make this slice even yummier (but less healthy!) replace the sultanas with chocolate drops.

Option

Replace the seeds, sultanas and rolled oats with two cups of untoasted muesli (may contain nuts).

Ingredients

- 125g butter
- ¾ cup raw sugar
- 2 Tbsp honey
- 1 cup flour
- 1 tsp baking powder
- 1 egg
- 2 Tbsp milk
- 4 Weet-Bix
- ⅓ cup sultanas
- ¼ cup pumpkin seeds
- ¼ cup sunflower seeds
- 2 Tbsp sesame seeds
- 1 cup rolled oats

1. Preheat oven to 180°C.
2. Melt butter, sugar and honey in the saucepan over a gentle heat, stirring occasionally. Do not boil.
3. Crush Weet-Bix into the large bowl, then add sultanas, seeds and rolled oats.
4. Sift flour and baking powder into the bowl. Mix all the dry ingredients together.
5. Crack the egg into the small bowl. Add milk and whisk to combine.
6. Add melted butter, sugar and honey mixture to bowl of dry ingredients, then add egg and milk mixture. Mix all together to combine.
7. Line baking tray with baking paper. Tip mixture into tray and push flat using wet fingertips.
8. Bake for 15–20 minutes, until golden.
9. While still warm, slice into 4cm x 4cm squares and place on rack to cool.
10. **EAT!**

Store the rest in an airtight container.

28 Sweets

Kids' Carrot Cake Muffins

MAKES 12

EQUIPMENT

- Sieve
- Large bowl
- Medium bowl
- Small bowl
- Grater
- Peeler
- Can opener
- Measuring cups
- Measuring spoons
- 12-hole muffin pan
- Wooden spoon
- Dessertspoon
- Wire rack
- Oven mitts

Ingredients

- 2 cups wholemeal flour
- 2 tsp baking powder
- 1 tsp ground cinnamon
- 2 medium carrots (about 100g each)
- 225g can crushed pineapple
- ⅓ cup raw sugar
- 2 Tbsp golden syrup
- 2 Tbsp oil
- 1 tsp baking soda
- 1 cup plain unsweetened yoghurt
- 1 egg
- Non-stick baking spray

These can be made ahead of time and stored in an airtight container for 2–3 days or frozen until needed.

1. Preheat oven to 180°C.
2. Sift flour, baking powder, cinnamon and salt into the large bowl. Some wheat bran from the flour will get stuck in the sieve; tip it into the bowl and then add the sugar.
3. Peel and grate carrots, add to the flour mixture and stir to combine.
4. Dissolve the baking soda in the yoghurt in the medium bowl. It will start to bubble and rise.
5. Put the egg, golden syrup and oil into the small bowl and stir to combine.
6. Drain the crushed pineapple, then add to the egg mixture and mix well.
7. Add all the ingredients to the large bowl and mix quickly; just enough to combine so all the flour is wet.
8. Spray muffin pans with non-stick cooking spray.
9. Use dessertspoon to spoon mixture evenly into muffin pans.
10. Bake for 12–15 minutes or until golden brown and cooked through.
11. Use the oven mitts to remove from the oven. Leave the muffins in the pan for 3 minutes before taking out and placing on rack to cool.
12. **EAT!**

nic says:
These muffins will keep you full for ages — lots of fibre and not too much sugar or oil!

Tip:
To test if your muffins are cooked, poke a skewer into the middle of one. If it comes out clean, they are ready, if it comes out sticky, they need to cook for a bit longer.

Sweets 31

I would like to thank Simon Gault and Brett McGregor for their support. Thanks to my photographer, Nigel Beach, all the wonderful people at Scholastic, and my mum.

Nic Brockelbank and Scholastic New Zealand Ltd are donating 50% of the royalties from sales of this book to the Muscular Dystrophy Association.

First published in 2013 by Scholastic New Zealand Limited
Private Bag 94407, Botany, Auckland 2163, New Zealand

Scholastic Australia Pty Limited
PO Box 579, Gosford, NSW 2250, Australia

Text © Nicholas Brockelbank, 2013

ISBN 978-1-77543-190-9

All rights reserved. No part of this publication may be reproduced or transmitted in any form or by any means, electronic, mechanical or digital, including photocopying, recording, storage in any information retrieval system, or otherwise, without prior written permission of the publisher.

National Library of New Zealand Cataloguing-in-Publication Data

Brockelbank, Nicholas, 2002-
Nic's lunchbox / by Nicholas Brockelbank ; photographs by Nigel Beach.
ISBN 978-1-77543-190-9
1.Lunchbox cooking—Juvenile literature. [1. Lunchbox cooking. 2. Cooking] I. Beach, Nigel. II. Title.
641.5123—dc 23

12 11 10 9 8 7 6 5 4 3 2   4 5 6 7 8 9 / 1

Publishing team: Lynette Evans, Diana Murray, Penny Scown and Frith Hughes
Photography: Nigel Beach
Designer: Book Design Ltd www.bookdesign.co.nz
Typeset in Bliss Light 11pt/14pt
Printed in Singapore by Tien Wah Press (PTE) Ltd

Scholastic New Zealand's policy, in association with Tien Wah Press, is to use papers that are renewable and made efficiently from wood grown in sustainable forests, so as to minimise its environmental footprint.